English Code S

Starter

Activity Book

Progress Chart

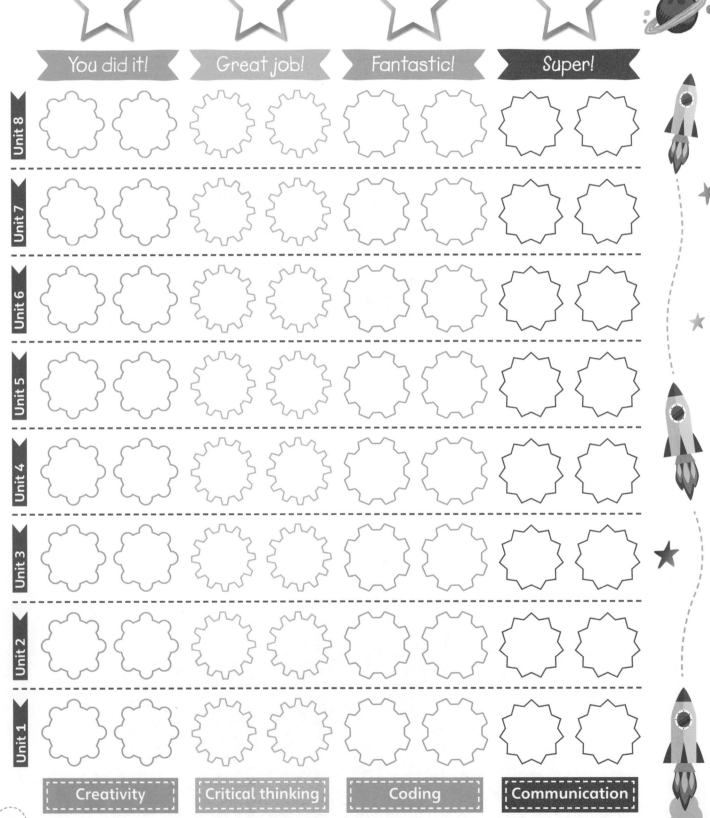

You did it!	Great job!	Fantastic!	Super!

Unit 8

Unit 7

Unit 6

Unit 5

Unit 4

Unit 3

Unit 2

Unit 1

Creativity	Critical thinking	Coding	Communication

Contents

Welcome!

 How can I enjoy my first day?

1 🎧 002 Listen and tick ☑. Then say.

1

2

3

4

2 🎧 003 Listen and sing. Then number the actions in order.

3 🎧 004 Listen and answer. Then ask and answer with a partner.

4 Look, count and colour. Then draw the missing dots.

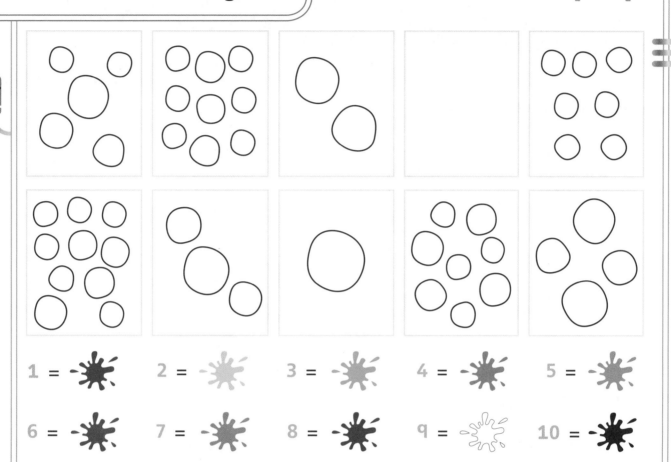

1 = ✴ 2 = ✴ 3 = ✴ 4 = ✴ 5 = ✴

6 = ✴ 7 = ✴ 8 = ✴ 9 = ✴ 10 = ✴

5 Listen and number in order.

Sam

Ana

Lui

Tina

6 Make your own name badge. Then say.

I can use greetings.

5

How can I make a birthday card?

I will learn colour and birthday words.

1 🎧 006 **Listen and tick ☑ .**

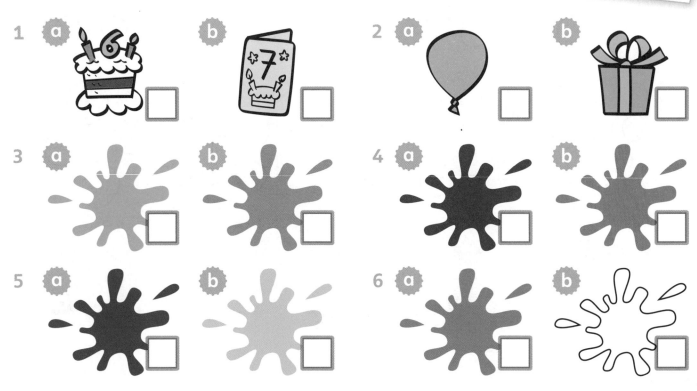

2 🎧 007 **Listen and sing. Number in order.**

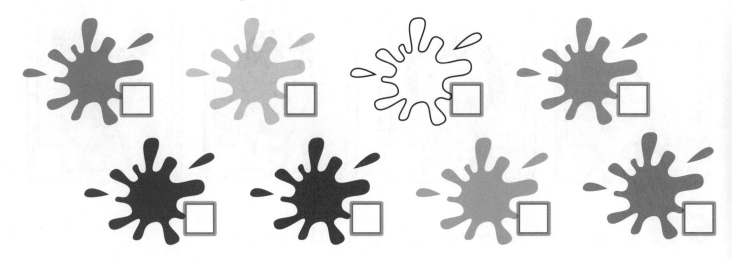

3 Look. Which items have not got a pair? Circle.

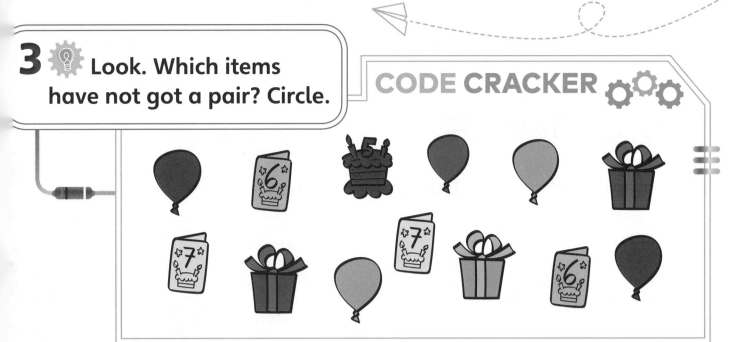

4 Look and say. Trace.

My picture dictionary!

blue   card   balloon   cake

EXTRA VOCABULARY

5 008 Listen, point and say.

I can use colour and birthday words.

Story lab

ENReanUISNG A STORY

ENJOYING A STORY

Hello FLUFFY!

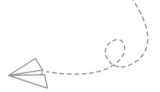

I will listen to a story about a birthday.

1 Remember the story. Number in order.

2 Listen and check your answers.

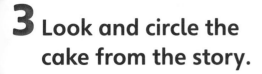
3 Look and circle the cake from the story.

CODE CRACKER

1 2 3 4 5

4 What do you think happens next in the story? Draw.

Values Take care of pets.

5 Tick ☑ or cross ☒.

1 2 3 4

I can listen to a story about a birthday.

Sound lab

I will learn the **c** and **b** sounds.

1 010 Colour and match. Then listen, point and say.

c c c c   b b b b

2 Colour and say.

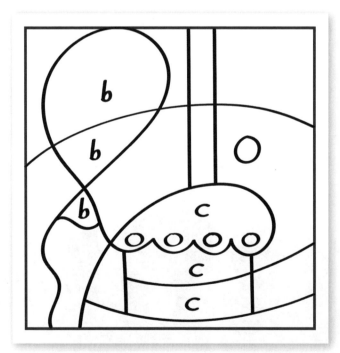

c =    b =

3 011 Listen and say.

I can use the **c** and **b** sounds.

I will learn about rainbows.

1 Colour the rainbow. Then say.

2 Look and match. Then listen and point.

3 Make a rainbow spinner.

I know about rainbows.

What's your favourite colour?

> I will ask and answer about favourite colours.

1 🎧 013 Listen and circle a or b. Then say.

1 a  b
2 a  b
3 a  b
4 a b

2 What number are the colours? Write.

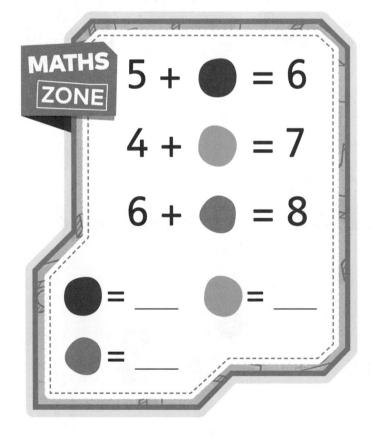

MATHS ZONE

$$5 + \bullet = 6$$

$$4 + \bullet = 7$$

$$6 + \bullet = 8$$

$\bullet =$ ___ $\bullet =$ ___

$\bullet =$ ___

3 Colour with your favourite colours. Play Bingo!

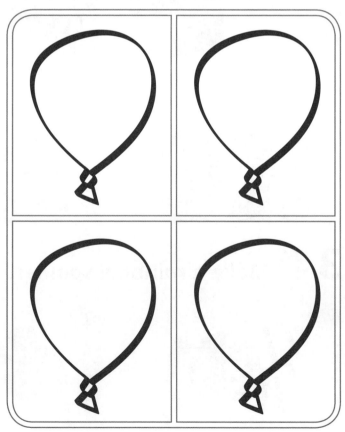

4 🎧 014 Listen and number.

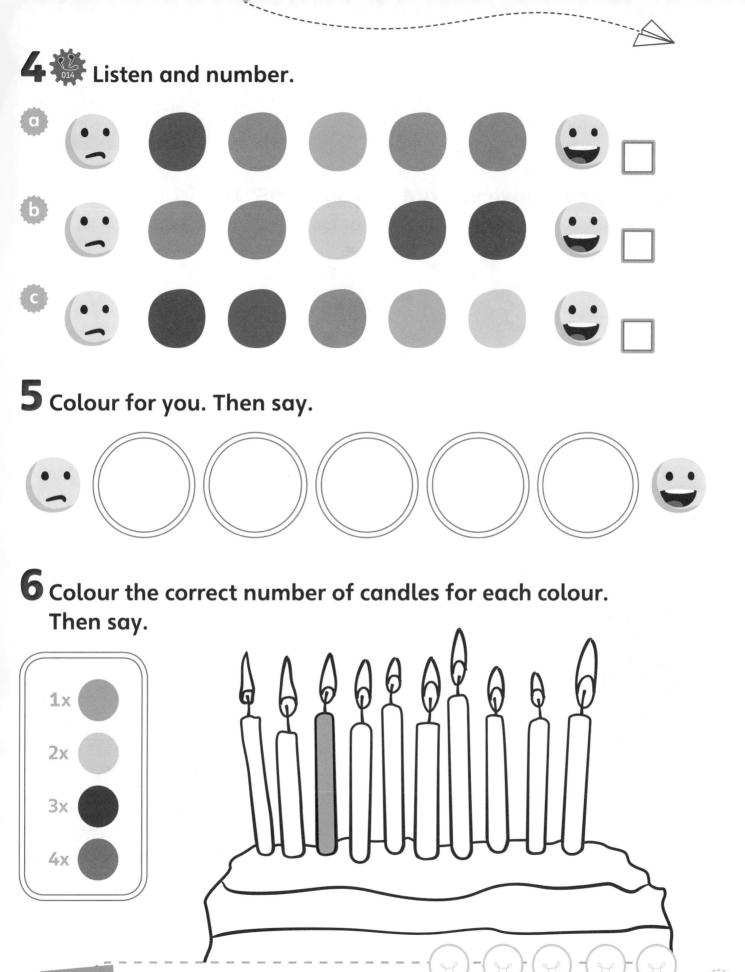

a

b

c

5 Colour for you. Then say.

6 Colour the correct number of candles for each colour.
   Then say.

1x
2x
3x
4x

Make a birthday card

Project report

1 What colours have you got on your card? Tick ☑.

2 Listen and point. Then complete your project report and draw.

My birthday card for

_____

3 Show your card to your family and friends.

I can make a birthday card.

1 🎧 016 Listen and draw the candles.

2 ❄ Draw and colour for you. Then say.

All about me!

Now go to your Progress Chart on page 2.

2 Mud kitchen

▷ How can I make table items for lunch?

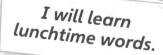

I will learn lunchtime words.

1 Match and say.

1  **2**  **3**  **4** **5**

2 🎧 017 Listen and sing. Tick ☑ the items you hear. What's missing?

 ☐  ☐  ☐ 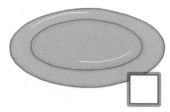 ☐

 ☐  ☐  ☐ 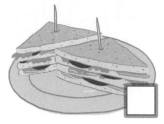 ☐

3 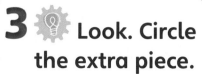 Look. Circle the extra piece.

4 Look and say. Trace.

My picture dictionary!

bowl

cup

spoon

plate

5  Listen, point and say.

I can use lunchtime words.

Story lab

ENTOYING A STORY

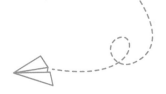

I will listen to a story about a play kitchen.

My mud kitchen

1 Remember the story. What's missing? Number, then draw.

2 Listen and check your answers.

3  Look, listen and tick ☑.

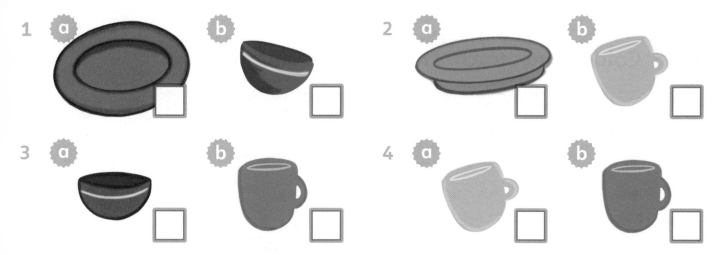

1 a   b ☐   2 a ☐   b ☐

3 a ☐   b ☐   4 a ☐   b ☐

4 Look and count. Then add.

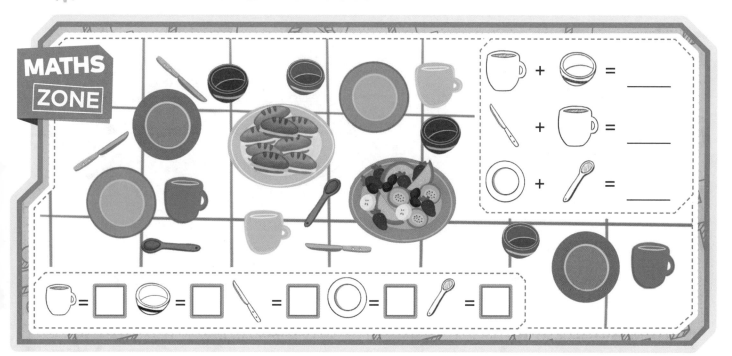

MATHS ZONE

🍵 + 🥣 = _____

🔪 + 🍵 = _____

🍽 + 🥄 = _____

🍵 = ☐   🥣 = ☐   🔪 = ☐   ◯ = ☐   🥄 = ☐

5 Colour for you.

  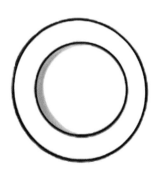

I will learn the s and p sounds.

1  Colour and match. Then listen, point and say.

2 Listen and tick ☑. Then say.

3 Say a tongue twister for picture 1.

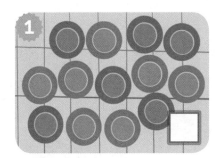 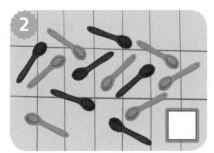

4 Look. Circle the odd one out.

CODE CRACKER

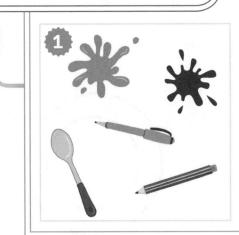  

I can use the s and p sounds.

Experiment lab

ART AND DESIGN: POTTERY

I will learn about pottery.

1 🔧 **Number in order. Listen and check. Then point and say.**

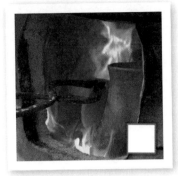   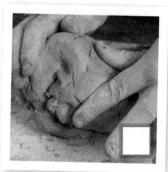

2 💡 **Look at the ways to make bowls. Match and say.**

1

2

3

3 ⚙️ **Try it out! Make the other bowls.**

I know about pottery.

Pass me a cup, please

1 🎧 024 Listen, play and tick ☑. Which *Bingo!* card wins?

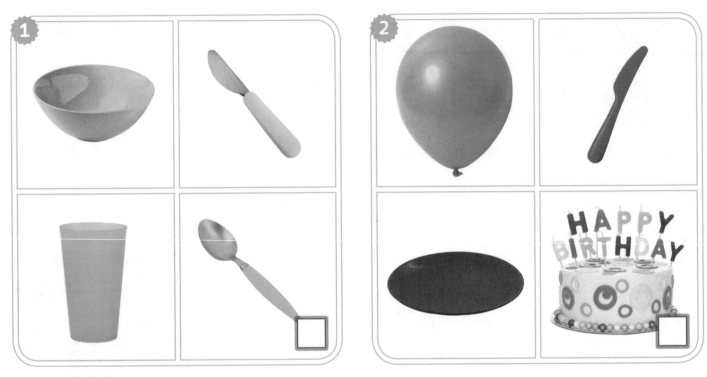

2 ⚙ Draw and play *Bingo!*

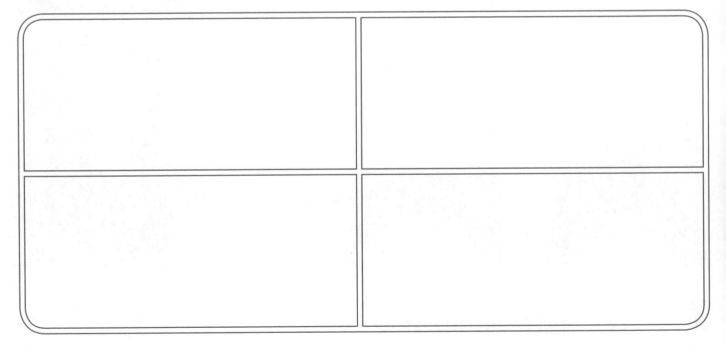

3 🎧 025 Listen and tick ☑.

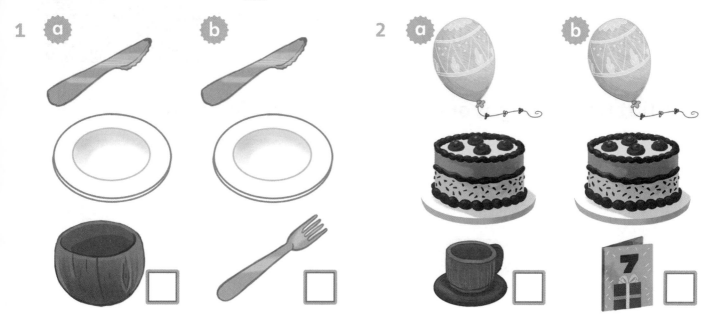

1   a   b

2   a   b

4 💬 Look at 3. Say with a friend.

Values   Ask politely.

5 🎧 026 Listen and circle 😀 or 🙁.

😀   🙁   😀   🙁

I can   ask for things politely.

Make table items for lunch

1 What have you got on your table? Tick ☑ and say.

2 🎧 027 Listen and point. Then complete your project report and draw.

3 Show your drawing in 2 to your family and friends. Then say.

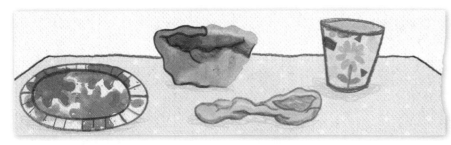

My table items: _____

_____ .

I can make table items for lunch.

1  Listen and tick ☑. Then say.

1 a b   2 a b

3 a b   4 a b

2 Draw and colour for you. Then say.

My lunch things!

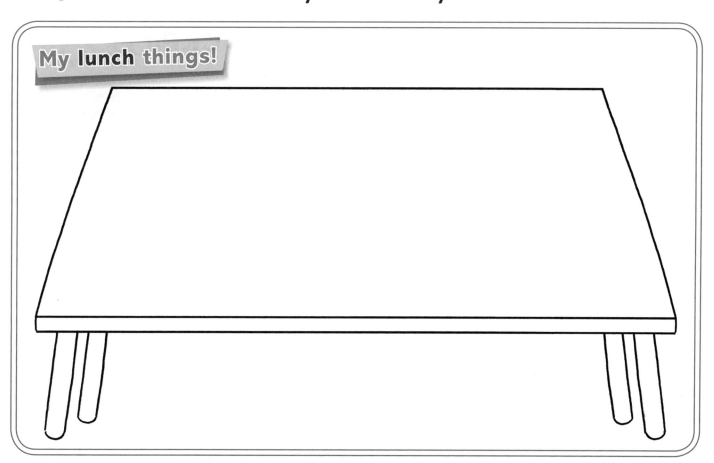

1 Checkpoint

1 Match and say.

2 Listen and draw paths. Then colour.

CODE CRACKER

3 Trace the letters.

balloon   card   plate   spoon   candle

1 Look and match. Then point and say.

2 What do you eat your lunch with? Tick ☑.

3 Continue the sequence. Say the colours.

4 What have you got in your lunchbox? Draw.

CODE CRACKER

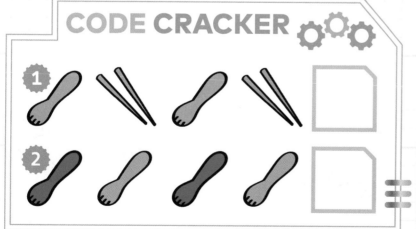

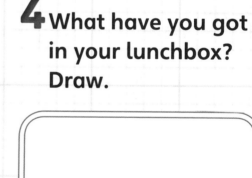

3 Music time!

How can I make a musical instrument?

1 🎧 030 Listen and tick ☑. Then point and say.

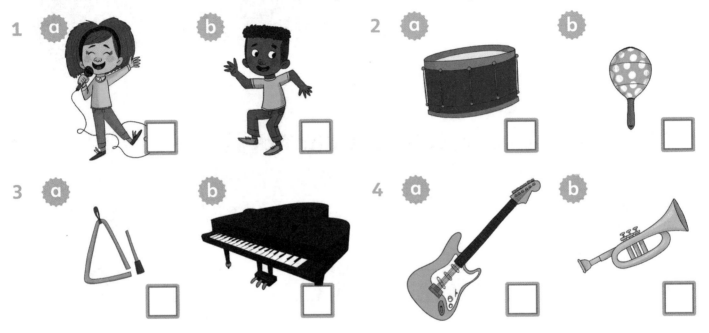

1 a   b   2 a   b

3 a   b   4 a   b

2 🎧 031 Listen and sing. Number in order.

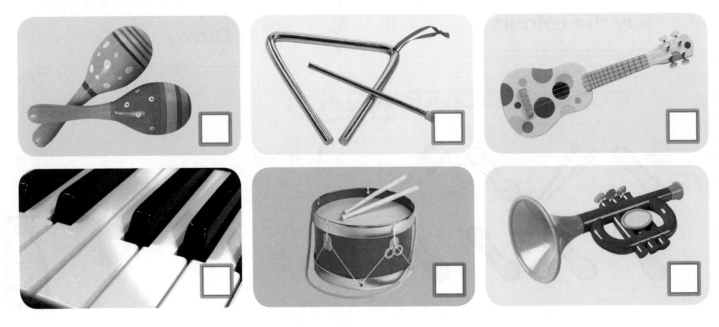

3 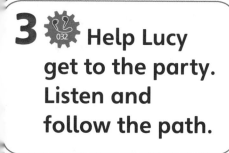 Help Lucy get to the party. Listen and follow the path.

4 Look and say. Trace.

My picture dictionary!

trumpet   drum   sing   piano

EXTRA VOCABULARY

5 Listen, point and say.

1   **2**   **3**

I can use musical instrument words.

Story lab

ENJOYING A STORY

I will listen to a story about music.

Play the drum, Fluffy!

1 Remember the story. Number in order.

2 🎧 034 Listen and check your answers.

3 🎧 035 Listen and point to the pictures.
Which ones are not music? Say.

4 🎧 036 Look and match. Then listen and check.

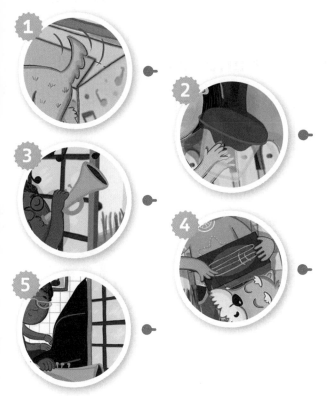

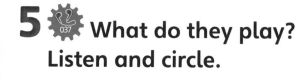

5 🎧 037 What do they play? Listen and circle.

6 ✏️ What do you want to play? Draw and say.

I can listen to a story about music.

Sound lab

I will learn the t and d sounds.

1 🎧 038 Colour and match. Then listen, point and say.

t t t   d d d

2 💡 What comes next? Look, tick ☑ and say.

3 🎧 039 Listen and follow. Then say.

CODE CRACKER ⚙⚙⚙

1

? =  ☐    ☐

2

? =  ☐

I can use the **t** and **d** sounds.

Experiment lab

SCIENCE: SOUND WAVES

I will learn about sound waves.

1 Listen and point.

2 Look and say. Then match.

①

②

③

3 Draw and colour the water.

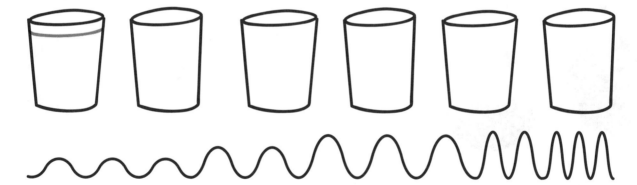

4 Look and listen. Then use two glasses and a pencil to copy the sounds.

I know about sound waves.

33

It's noisy!

COMMUNICATION

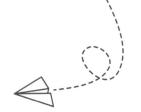

I will talk about musical sounds.

1 042 Listen and circle. Then say.

2 Look, sort and draw lines. Then say.

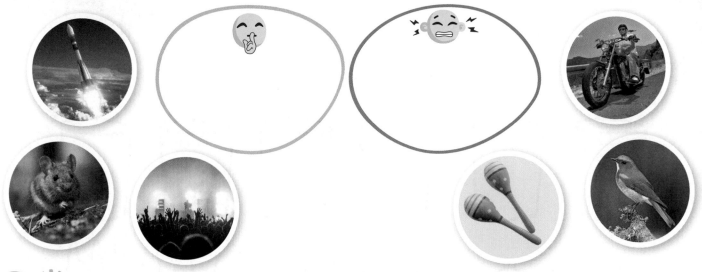

3 Draw two quiet things and two noisy things.

4 Look, count and write.

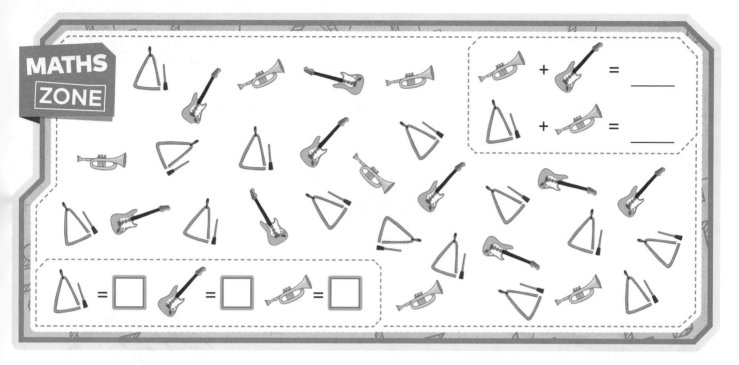

MATHS ZONE

5 🎧 043 Listen. Then play the game.

Listen to each other.

6 Do you listen to your teacher and your friends? Colour.

I can talk about musical sounds.

PROJECT AND REVIEW UNIT 3

Make a musical instrument

1 **What have you got on your table? Tick ☑ and say.**

1

2

3

4

5

6

2 **Listen and point. Then complete your project report and draw.**

044

My musical instrument
is a _____ .

3 **Show your instrument to your family and friends.**

I can make a musical instrument.

1 🎧 045 Listen and number.

a

b

c

d

e

f

2 ✨ Draw you and your favourite instrument. Then say.

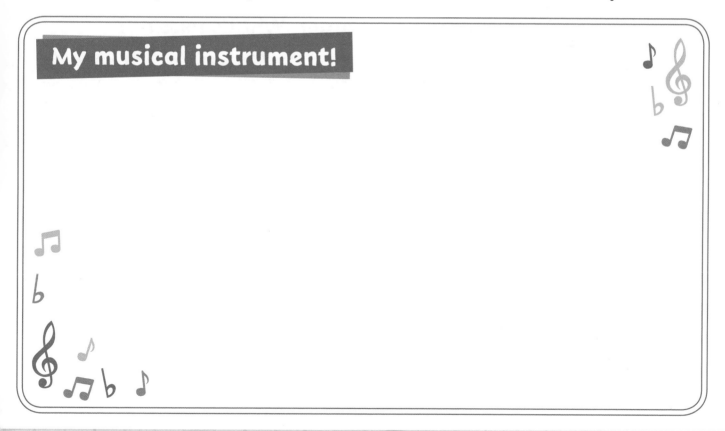

My musical instrument!

4 At the farm

➤ **How can I make a toy farm?**

> *I will learn farm words.*

1 Follow and tick ☑. Then say.

1 a b 2 a b

3 a b 4 a b

2 046 Listen and sing. Number in order. What's missing?

3 💡 Continue the sequence. Then say.

CODE CRACKER

4 Look and say. Trace.

My picture dictionary!

fox   sheep   cow   tractor

EXTRA VOCABULARY

5 🎧 047 Listen, point and say.

I can use farm words.

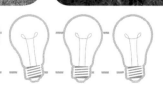

39

Story lab

ENJOYING A STORY

I will listen to a story about a fox.

The red fox

1 Remember the story. What's missing? Number, then draw.

2 Listen and check your answers.

3 What do they eat in the story? Match and say.

4 🎧 049 Listen and tick ☑. Then say.

5 Count, calculate and draw. Then say.

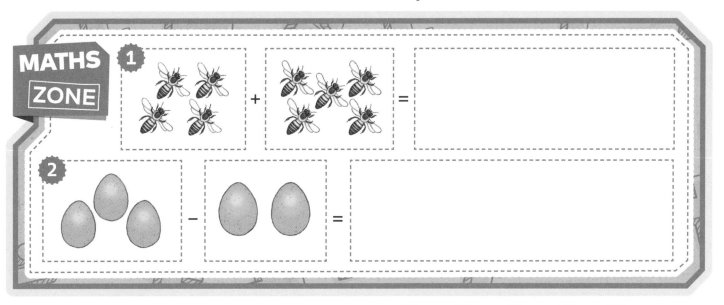

MATHS ZONE

I can listen to a story about a fox.

Sound lab

A AND F

I will learn the **a** and **f** sounds.

1 🎧 050 **Colour and match. Then listen, point and say.**

2 🎧 051 **Listen and tick ☑. Then say.**

1  ☐

2  ☐

3 🎨 **Say a tongue twister for picture 1.**

4 💡 **Find the path. Then colour and say.**

CODE CRACKER

ⓐ → ⓟ → ⓒ → ⓕ

I can use the **a** and **f** sounds.

I will learn about food from animals.

1 🎧 052 Match and say. Then listen and check.

2 💡 Think and draw.

 →

 →

 →

3 💡 Think about your experiment. Then order.

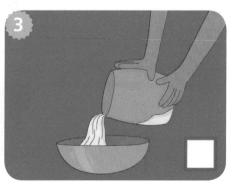

I know about food from animals.

43

Shut the gate!

COMMUNICATION

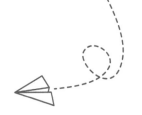

1 🎧 053 Listen and tick ☑.

1 ⓐ ⓑ   2 ⓐ ⓑ

3 ⓐ ⓑ   4 ⓐ ⓑ

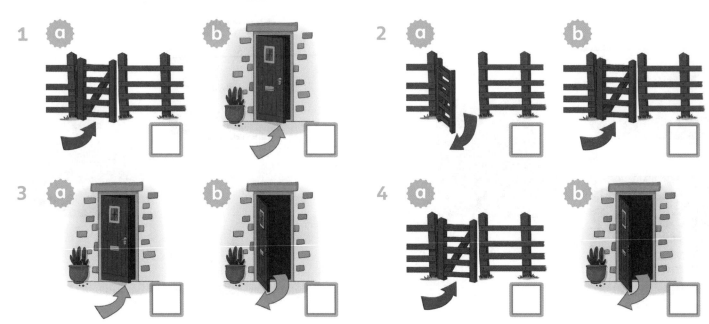

2 🎧 054 Listen and tick ☑ the correct sequence.

3  Look and say a sequence from 2.

4  Number in order. Watch the video again to check.

5 Make a gate. Act out the video with a friend.

6 Look and circle 😃 or ☹.

I can give instructions.

1 What have you got on your farm? Write the number.

2 🎧 055 Listen and point. Then complete your project report and draw.

This is my _____ .

3 Show your drawing in 2 to your family and friends.

I can make a toy farm.

1 🎧 056 Listen and write the numbers.

2 ✸ Draw and colour for you. Then say.

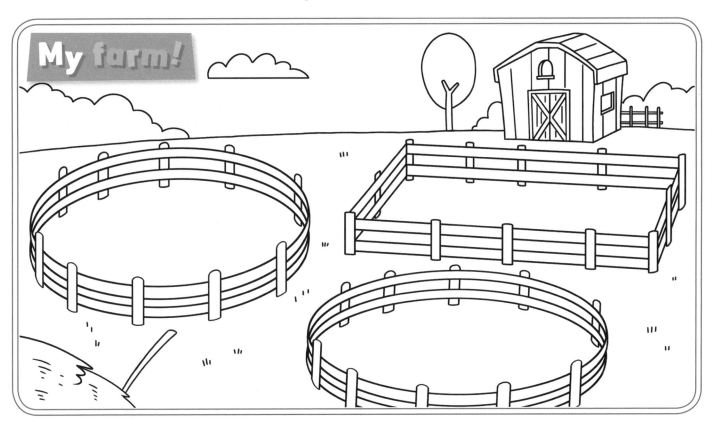

My farm!

2 Checkpoint

1 Say the words. Then circle the odd one out.

2 Listen and trace the paths.

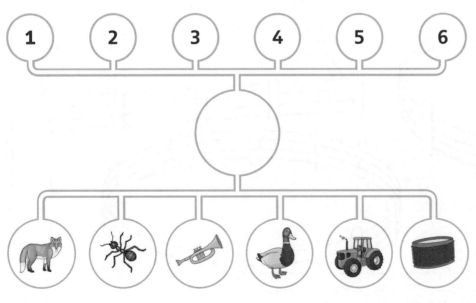

3 Draw a path in 2. Say.

4 Trace the letters.

ant

drum

fox

tractor

1 🎧 058 Listen and number. Then act out.

2 🎧 059 What animals are in the songs? Listen and tick ☑.

1 a    b    2 a    b

3 a    b   4 a    b

3 What songs do you know about animals? Tell a friend.

4 Play your musical instrument. Tell and share.

5 My dinosaur

How can I make a dinosaur puzzle?

I will learn dinosaur words.

1 What have they got? Match and say.

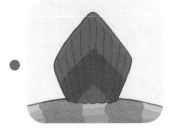
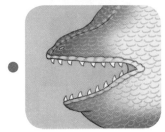

2 Listen and sing. Number in order. Draw another action from the song.

3 Look and follow the arrows. Where does Fluffy go?

CODE CRACKER

4 Look and say. Trace.

My picture dictionary!

lizard   tail   legs   spikes

5 Listen, point and say. Then sing and do the actions.

1    2    3    4

I can use dinosaur words.

Story lab

ENERGING A STORY
ENJOYING A STORY

It's a dinosaur!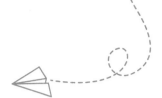

1 Remember the story. Number in order.

2 Listen and check your answers.

3 🎧 063 Listen and circle.

1	a / **b**	2	a / **b**
3	a / b	4	a / **b**
5	a / b	6	a / **b**

4 💬 Draw 2 animals. Play the game from 3 with a partner.

a

b

5 💡 Find four differences. Then say.

Sound lab

I will learn the **l** and **e** sounds.

1 Trace and match. Then listen, point and say.

lizard   elephant   legs   egg

2 Look and write **l** or **e**. Then say.

1

2

____l____ unch   ____ ____ gs

3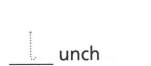

4

____ ____ bow   ____ ____ ____ phant

3 Colour and say.

l =    e =

I can use the **l** and **e** sounds.

Experiment lab

SCIENCE: WHAT DINOSAURS EAT

1 🎧 065 Listen. Then look and match.

2 💡 Look, sort and draw lines.

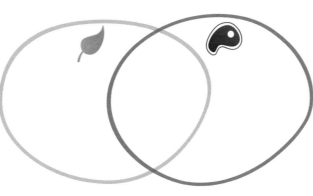

3 ❄ Draw more animals for each section in 2.

4 ❄ Make clothes peg dinosaurs. Then play and say.

I know about what dinosaurs eat.

Is it a dinosaur?

COMMUNICATION

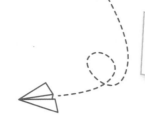

I will give support to my friends.

1  Listen and tick ☑.

2 Listen and draw. Then compare with a partner.

3 Think of an animal. Describe to a partner. The partner draws.

It's got 4 legs.

4 Look, count and write.

MATHS ZONE

☐

☐

☐ x ☐ = ☐

☐ x ☐ = ☐

5 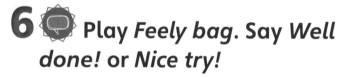 **What's in the bag? Listen and circle.**

6 💬 **Play *Feely bag*. Say *Well done!* or *Nice try!***

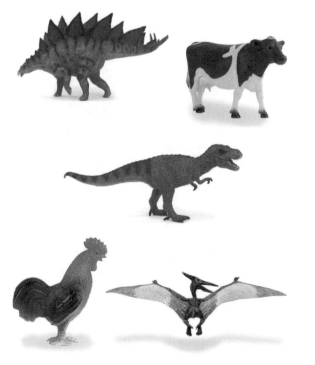

I can give support to my friends.

1 What has your dinosaur got? Tick ☑.

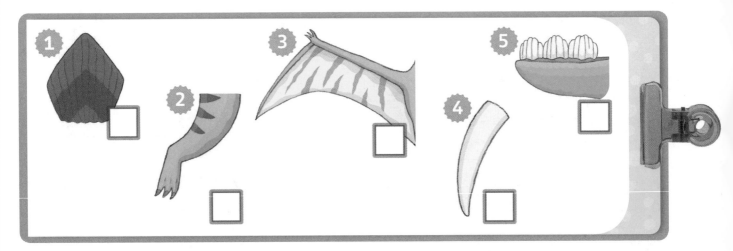

2 Complete your project report. Then draw.

My dinosaur has got

_____

_____ .

3 Do your puzzle with family and friends.

I can make a dinosaur puzzle.

1 Circle the odd one out. Then say.

1

2

3

4

2 Draw your favourite dinosaur. Then say.

My favourite dinosaur!

6 A picnic

How can we have a picnic?

I will learn picnic words.

1 🎧069 Listen and tick ☑. Then say.

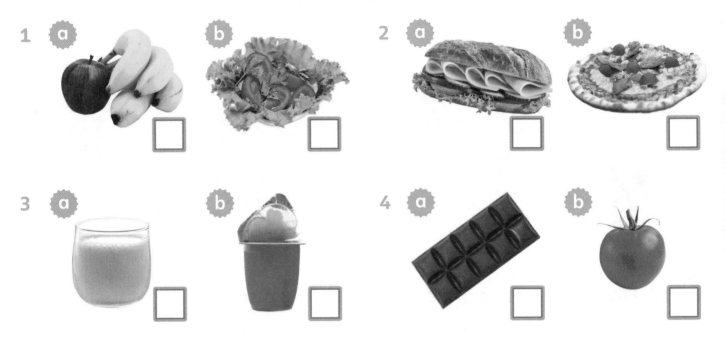

1 a   b   2 a   b

3 a   b   4 a   b

2 🎧070 Listen and sing. Listen to verse 1 and tick ☑ the picnic.

3 🎧 071 Listen and number.

a

b

c

d

4 Look and say. Trace.

My picture dictionary!

yoghurt   pizza   fruit   salad

5 🎧 072 Listen, point and say.

1

2

3

4

I can use picnic words.

Story lab

ENJOYING A STORY

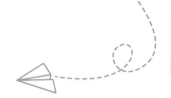

I will listen to a story about a picnic.

Picnic time

1 Remember the story. What's missing? Number, then draw.

2 Listen and check your answers.

3 💡 Look and tick ☑ the food from the story. Then say.

4 ☎ Listen and draw 😀 or 😞. Then say.

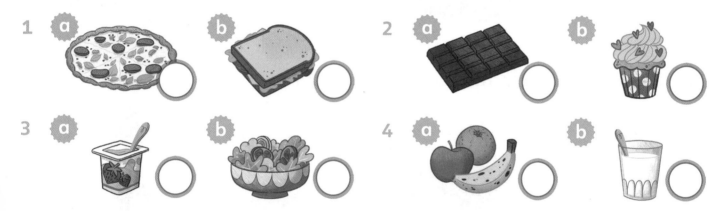

Values Learn to share.

5 What can you share? Tick ☑.

6 💥 What do you like at a picnic? Draw.

Sound lab

> **I will learn the y and j sounds.**

1 🎧 075 Trace and match. Then listen, point and say.

yo-yo   yellow   jug   jar

2 🎧 076 Listen and circle the correct letter.

1
y / j

2
y / j

3
y / j

4
y / j

3 Circle the odd one out.

1

2

I can use the y and j sounds.

64

I will learn about sugar.

1 🔧 Remember and match. Then listen and check.

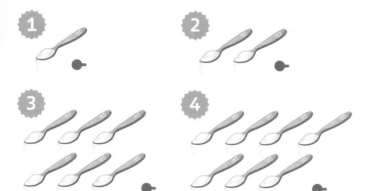

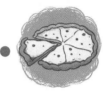

2 💡 Look at the items in 1. Calculate the sugar.

3 💡 Look and complete the bar graph.
Use your Experiment time results.

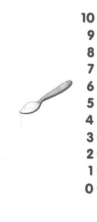

I know about sugar.

Wash your hands!

COMMUNICATION

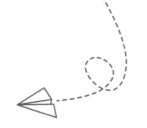

I will give instructions.

1 🎧 078 **Listen and tick ☑.**

2 ▶ **Say and number in order. Watch the video again to check.**

3 When do you wash your hands? Tick ☑ and say.

4 Decorate a soap dispenser.

5 Listen, chant and act out.

I can give instructions.

Have a picnic

Project report

1 **What have you got in your picnic? Tick ☑.**

2 **Complete your project report. Then draw.**

In my picnic I have got

_____ .

3 🔊 080 **Listen and repeat. Show your drawing in 2 to your family and friends.**

I can have a picnic.

1 🎧 081 Listen and tick ☑ the food at the picnic.
Then listen again and circle.

2 ⚙ Draw and colour for you. Then say.

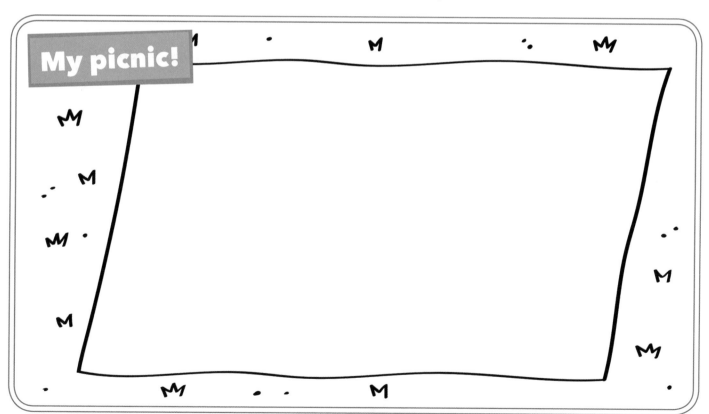

My picnic!

Now go to your Progress Chart on page 2.

3 Checkpoint

1 Look and sort. Add more items.

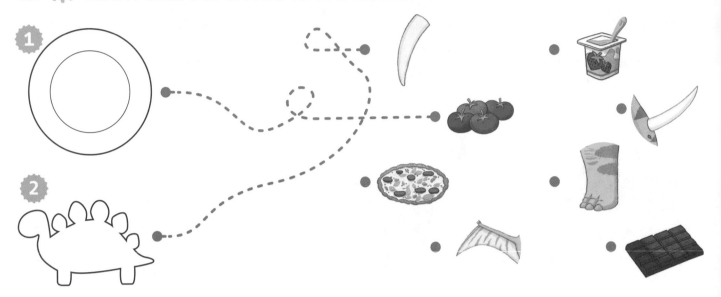

2 Listen and trace the paths.

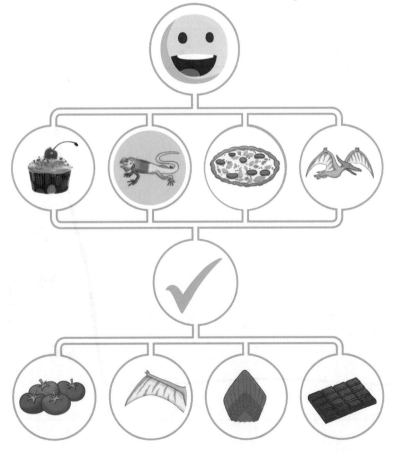

3 Look and write.

> cake   dinosaurs
> lizards   pizza

I  _____ .

I  _____ .

I  _____ .

I  _____ .

1 💡 **Look and match. Point and say.**

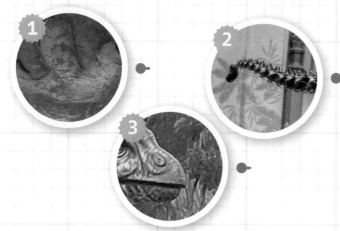

2 🎧 083 **Listen and tick ☑.**

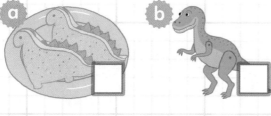

3 🎨 **Draw food for your dinosaur picnic. Tell and share.**

7 Under the sea

I will learn sea animal words.

1 Match and say.

  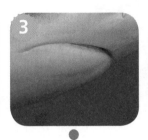 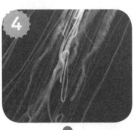 

1 2 3 4 5

2 What's missing from 1? Draw and say.

3 Listen and sing. Colour the fish in order.

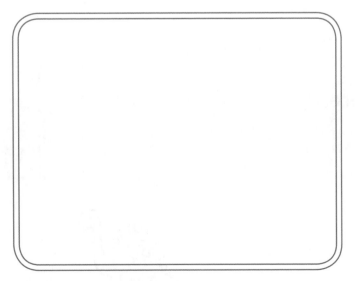

4 Which animals are not a pair? Circle.

5 Look and say. Write the first letter.

My picture dictionary!

___rab   ___hark   ___hrimp   ___ellyfish

EXTRA VOCABULARY

6 Listen, point and say.

I can use sea animal words.

Story lab

ENJOYING A STORY

I will listen to a story about sea animals.

Can you see teeth?

1 Remember the story. Number in order.

2 🎧 086 Listen and check your answers.

3 Listen and tick ☑.

4 Listen and draw.

5 Draw a fish tank in your notebook.
Ask and answer with a partner.

 listen to a story about sea animals.

I will learn the **i** and **u** sounds.

1 🔧 089 **Write, trace and match. Then listen, point and say.**

___p   ___nsect   ___mbrella   ___gloo

2 💡 **Which two match? Circle.**

CODE CRACKER

3 🔧 090 **Listen, point and say.**

I can use the **i** and **u** sounds.

Experiment lab

I will learn about animals with shells.

1 Tick ☑ the animals with shells.

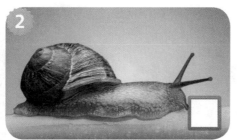

2 Look, sort and draw lines.

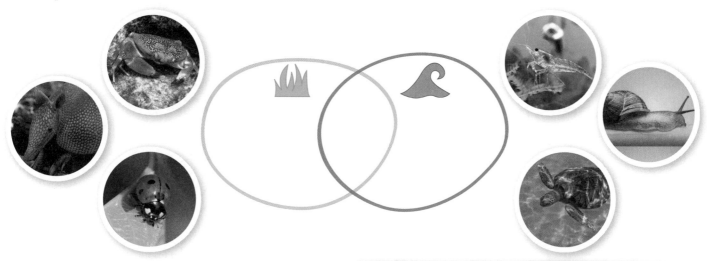

3 Draw more animals for each section in 2.

4 Make a shell crab.

I know about animals with shells.

77

It's windy!

COMMUNICATION

I will talk about the weather.

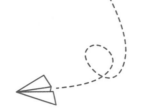

1 🎧 091 Listen and tick ☑.

1
 a
 b

2
 a
 b

3
 a
 b

4
 a
 b

2 💡 Continue the sequence. Then say.

CODE CRACKER

1

2

3

3 Are the children wearing the correct clothes?
Look and tick ☑ or cross ☒. Then say.

4 Make dressing-up dolls.

5 Play with your dolls and say.

It's hot!

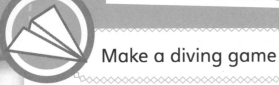

Make a diving game

Project report

1 What does your diving game have? Tick ☑.

2 🌀 Complete your project report. Then draw.

My diving tank has _____

_____ .

3 🎧 Listen and say. Play your game with friends and family.

I can make a diving game.

1 Listen. What's on the tray? Tick ☑ or cross ☒.

2 Draw your favourite sea animals. Then say.

My favourite sea animals!

Now go to your Progress Chart on page 2.

How can I act out a story?

1 💡 Match and say.

1

2

3

4

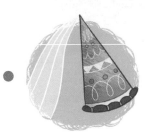

2 🎧 094 Listen and sing. Number in order.

3 Continue the sequence. Then say.

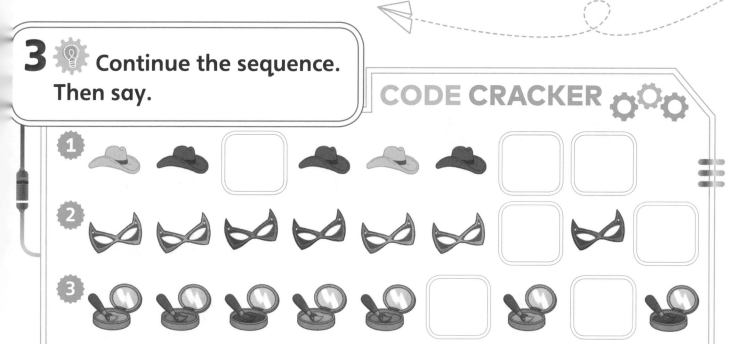

4 Look and say. Write the first letter. Trace.

My picture dictionary!

____ask ____owgirl ____irate ____at

5 Listen, point and say.

I can use fancy dress words.

Story lab

ENexp ENJOYING A STORY

I'm the pirate! ⚓

1 Remember the story. What's missing? Number, then draw.

2 🎧 096 **Listen and check your answers.**

3 What do they wear in the story? Match and say.

4 🔧 097 **Listen and tick** ☑. **Then say.**

5 💡 **Look, think and draw.**

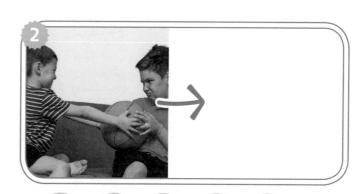

I can listen to a story about a pirate.

Sound lab

I will learn the **m** and **o** sounds.

1 Trace and match. Then listen, point and say.

orange   mask   ostrich   milk

2 Look and write **m** and **o**. Then say.

d ____ g   dru ____   ____ ask   f ____ x

3 Find the path. Then colour and say.

CODE CRACKER

o → j → e → y → l

I can use the **m** and **o** sounds.

Experiment lab

I will learn about making wool.

1 Number in order. Listen and check. Then say.

2 What animals can you get wool from? Tick ☑.

3 Do finger knitting.

I know about making wool.

I'm happy!

COMMUNICATION

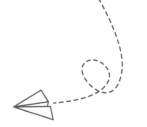
I will talk about feelings.

1 Listen and number.

a   ☐

b   ☐

c   ☐

d   ☐

2 Look and circle. Then say.

3 How do you feel in each place? Look, draw and say.

4 Complete and say.

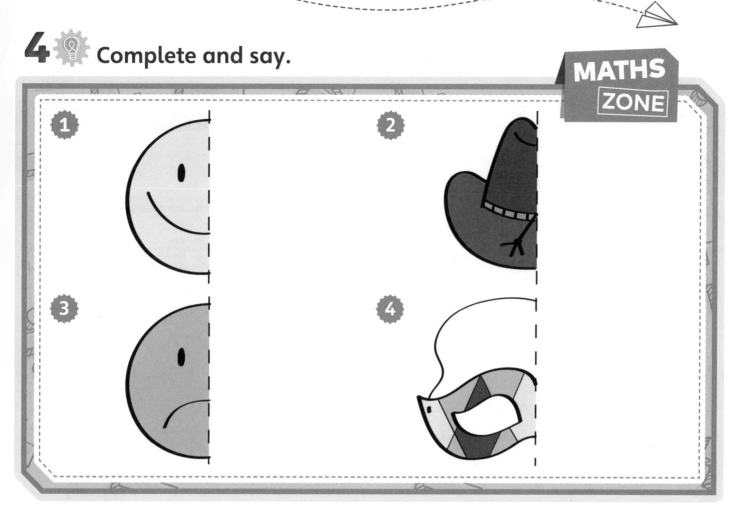

1 **2** **3** **4**

5 Make a superhero mask. Think of your superhero name and say.

I can talk about feelings.

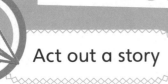

Act out a story

Project report

1 What is your finger puppet wearing? Tick ☑.

2 Complete your project report. Then draw.

3 101 Listen and say. Show your drawing in **2** to your family and friends.

My finger puppet is wearing

_____ .

I can act out a story.

1 Find five differences. Then say.

2 Draw and colour for you and a friend. Then say.

My costume!

4 Checkpoint

1 Circle sea animals in blue and costumes in green. Then say.

2 Listen and trace. Then say.

3 Look and write.

a costume   a hat
a mask   face paints

1 I'm _____

_____ .

2 I'm _____

_____ .

3 I'm _____

_____ .

4 I'm _____

_____ .

Culture 4
SEASIDE FESTIVALS

1 💡 **Look and match. Point and say.**

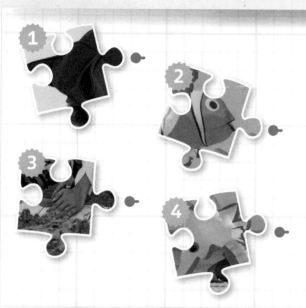

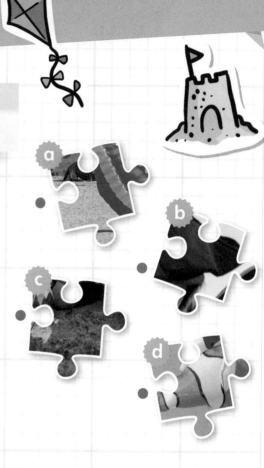

2 💡 **Sort. Then compare with a friend.**

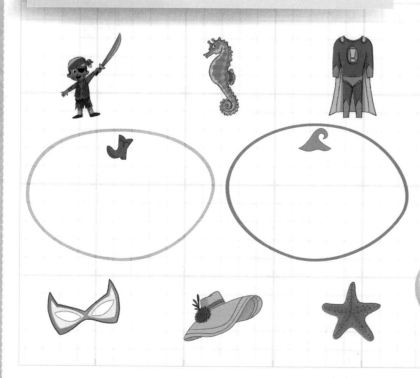

3 **Fly your kite! Tell and share.**

OUR WORLD

INTRO:

Here we stand: children of every age,
This is our world and the world's our stage.
We can laugh, we can cry — we can float, we can fly,
We can dance, we can sing — we can do almost anything
in OUR world ... our *beautiful* world.

VERSE 1:

Some of us are small; some of us are tall,
Some of us are shy; some say hi to everybody,
Some of us like numbers; some of us love words,
Some of us watch football, and some of us watch the birds!

(CHORUS)

This is *our* world ... we're different but the same.
We live and learn together — we get to know each other ...
in OUR world ... our *beautiful* world.

VERSE 2:

Some of us like music; some of us like cars,
Some of us draw pictures, looking at the stars,
Some of us are scientists, trying to find the code,
All of us can help a friend and give a hand to hold.

This is *our* world — there's room for everyone.
We learn to live together, and we have a lot of fun ...
In **our** world ... in **our** world ... in our beautiful world!

A a   B b   C c   D d   E e

F f   G g   H h   I i   J j

K k   L l   M m   N n   O o

P p   Q q   R r   S s   T t   U u

V v   W w   X x   Y y   Z z

Pearson Education Limited
KAO TWO
KAO Park
Hockham Way
Harlow, Essex
CM17 9SR
England
and Associated Companies throughout the world.

english.com/englishcode

First published 2021
Eighth impression 2024
ISBN: 978-1-292-32287-2
Set in Heinemann Roman 16.5 pt
Printed in Slovakia by Neografia

Acknowledgements

The publishers and author(s) would like to thank the following people and institutions for their feedback and comments during the development of the material:

Argentina

Maria Belen Gonzalez Milbrandt (Director Colegio Sol De Funes), Alejandra Garre (Coordinator Colegio San Patricio), Patricia Bettucci (Teacher Colegio Verbo Encarnado), Colegio Los Arroyos (Coordinator Luciana Pittondo), Instituto Stella Maris (Coordinator Ana Maria Ferrari), Gabriela Dichiara (Coordinator Nivel Pre-Primario En Escuela Normal N° 1 Dr Nicolas Avellaneda), Alejandra Ferreyra & Maria Elena Casals (Profesor Escuela Normal N° 1 Dr Nicolas Avellaneda), Maria Julia Occhi (Primary Director Colegio San Bartolomé Sede Fisherton), Gisele Manzur (English Director- Colegio Educativo Latinoamericano), Griselda Rodriguez (Ex-Directora de Instituto IATEL), Cultural Inglesa de Santa Fe (Olga Poloni y Silvia Cantero), Escuela Primaria de la Universidad Nacional del Litoral (Santa Fe) (Ricardo Noval, Natalia Mártirez y Romina Papini), Colegio La Salle Jobson Santa Fe (Santa Fe) (Miriam Ibañez), Colegio de la Inmaculada Concepción (Santa Fe) (Gabriela Guglielminetti), Colegios Niño Jesús y San Ezequiel Moreno (Santa Fe) (Ivana Serrano), Advice Prep School (Santa Fe) (Virginia Berutti), Centro de Enseñanza de Inglés Mariana G. Puygros (Santa Fe). Focus Group Participants: Alejandra Aguirre (Coordinator Colegio Español), Alicia Ercole (Director Instituto CILEL (Casilda)), Marianella Robledo (Coordinator Insituto CILEL (Casilda)), Viviana Valenti (Director Instituto Let's Go), Natalia Berg (Prof. Colegio de La Paz (San Nicolás)).

Turkey

Ugur Okullari, Isik Okullari, Doğa Koleji, Fenerbahce Koleji, Arı Okullari, Maya Okullari, Yükselen Koleji, Pinar Koleji, Yeşilköy Okullari, Final Okullari, Vizyon Koleji

Image Credits:

123RF.com: aivolie 11, Aleksandr Belugin 16, 16, Alexander 41, Alongkon Suntorn 83, Anatoli Kosolapov 38, Anatolii Tsekhmister 38, 59, 59, 59, Blaj Gabriel 4, Corey A Ford 73, damedeeso 22, David Steele 49, Derrick Neill 55, digieye 61, Dmitry Kalinovsky 61, dolgachoc 34, donatas1205 16, 16, Elena Nichizhenova 83, firina 26, Frederic Prochasson 46, 49, 49, 55, 87, Ian Stewart 41, Ijupco 17, irochka 43, joannawnuk 21, Jozef Polc 67, Konstantin Shaklein 34, kritchanut 79, loraliu 86, Lubos Kovalik 41, Lubos Kovalik/ 46, Lucian Milasan 11, Malgorzata Litkowska 72, 72, 80, mitarart 21, nyul 24, Phana Sitti 27, 27, pixelrobot 86, rido 90, Ruth Black 63, Sataporn Jiwjalaen 16, 26, Sean Lema 77, sevaljevic 87, tiwaz 57, tobi 61, Winai Tepsuttinun 67, Yaroslav Kryuchka 57; **Alamy Stock Photo:** Islandstock 93, 93; **Getty Images:** AGEphotography/iStock/Getty Images Plus 89, AGEphotography/iStock/Getty Images Plus 87, AMR Image/iStock/Getty Images Plus 72, 72, 80, Anastasiis Boriagina/iStock/Getty Images Plus 89, Andyd/E+ 27, Anna Pekunova 21, bazilfoto/iStock/Getty Images Plus 38, by Chakarin Wattanamongkol/Moment 87, cdascher/iStock/Getty Images Plus 72, 72, 80, cheche22 27, Choreograph/iStock/Getty Images Plus 83, clubfoto/iStock/Getty Images Plus 26, damnura/iStock/Getty Images Plus 46, Doctor_bass/iSTock/Getty Images Plus 88, EcoPic/iStock/Getty Images Plus 46, Erstudiostok/iStock/Getty Images Plus 46, EyeEm 77, fizkes/iStock/Getty Images Plus 80, fstop123/iStock/Getty Images Plus 83, George Doyle/Stockbyte 79, Granger Wootz 88, Imgorthand 93, IrinaBort/iStock/Getty Images Plus 16, iStockphoto 28, 43, 43, 54, John Lawson, Belhaven/Moment 41, Johner RF 87, Jonathan Kirn 54, 54, Jose Luis Pelaez Inc/Digital Vision 58, Kraig Scarbinsky/Photodisc 83, Linka a Odom/Stone 34, Ljupco/iStock/Getty Images Plus 79, Llgorko/iStock/Getty Images Plus 27, loco75/iStock/Getty Images Plus 34, mauribo/iStock/Getty Images Plus 49, michaeljung/iStock/Getty Images Plus 68, Mike Kemp 79, 79, MITO images 78, 78, Nick David/Photodisc 83, p_ponomareva/iStock/

Getty Images Plus 24, Paffy69/iStock/Getty Images Plus 79, Peter Cade/Stone 41, Photoevent 60, 68, PhotoObjects.net/Getty Images Plus 57, Picsfive/iStock/Getty Images Plus 80, Prykhodov/iStock/Getty Images Plus 57, robtek 60, 68, s-cphoto/E+ 26, Tatiana Syrtseva/iStock/Getty Images Plus 61, Tetra Images 43, 60, 68, Tetra Images - PT Images 78, Ziva_K/iStock/Getty Images Plus 79, 79; **Louisa Leitao:** 21; **Pearson Education Ltd:** Alice McBroom 90, Coleman Yuen 36, Jon Barlow 36, 46, 47, 49, 50; Rafal Trubisz 33, Trevor Clifford 56, Tudor Photography 57, 67, 81; **Shutterstock. com:** 7th Son Studio 28, aabeele 86, aastock 80, AdrianNunez 64, Africa Studio 16, 22, 24, 27, 63, 79, AISPIX 78, Alexander Sviridov 83, alexsvirid 83, AlinaMD 88, Alter-ego 64, 64, 64, amphaiwan 22, 24, Anastasia Shilova 4, Andrea Izzotti 73, Andrew F.Kazmierski 79, Andrey Eremin 22, 24, AnEduard 54, artjazz 81, artphotoclub 60, 68, Arve Bettum 63, Bence Sibalin 80, Berents 64, 64, Blaj Gabriel 4, BlueOrange Studio 76, Brandon Alms 73, Cheryl Casey 83, ConstantinosZ 28, CreativeNature.nl 34, Daniel Prudek 38, 38, 59, DenisNata 79, Dikky Oesin 49, Dominique de La Croix 86, Dotted Yeti 55, Durden Images 49, Dustin Dennis 43, Elena Schweitzer 28, 32, Elnur 83, Eric Isselee 38, 38, Erika Cross 4, ESB Professional 68, Ethan Daniels 77, Eve Photography 49, Four Oaks/Shutterstock 54, 54, 87, Francesco De Marco 87, Geanina Bechea 46, 49, 49, 53, GraphicRN 53, GraphicWorlds 39, Gregory Johnston/Shutterstock 78, GroovyGloryPhoto 34, Guenter Albers 11, 11, Heidi Schneider 28, HelloRF Zcool 16, hermitis 78, 78, Hilomo 11, Ian Rentoul 49, 59, Ikordela 11, J. Helgason 22, Jamie Hall 86, JDCarballo 54, 59, Jiang Hongyan 57, Jim Lopes 78, JOAT 21, Johan Swanepoel 77, 77, Kaiskynet Studio 81, Kateryna Biatolva 11, Kateryna Omelianchenko 21, Ken stocker 71, 71, Kletr 17, Kuttelvaserova Stuchelova 77, Kwadrat 39, Lamyai 87, Lee Thompson Images 64, 64, Ljupco Smokovski 34, Luis Molinero 4, Lukas Gojda 3, Manuel M Almeida 81, Marcin Sywia Ciesielski 49, Marcos del Mazo 77, Marie C Fields 61, Marijus Auruskevicius 21, Massimo Todaro 71, 71, Max Topchii 46, Maxx-Studio 17, michaeljung 46, Michel Cecconi 76, Michelle Pacitto 80, mlorenz 77, Nakornthai 76, Nanette Grebe 4, Neirfy 79, NeydtStock 22, 26, Nik Merkulov 86, nortongo 16, Odon Arianna 11, oksana2010 63, Palto 77, Panatda Saengow 57, Panu Ruangjan 34, Patryk Kosmider/Shutterstock 60, PavelSvoboda 11, Photo Melon 33, Photoroyalty 83, Picsfive 54, 57, Proartphoto 24, 26, Prostock-studio 14, Rattana 71, 71, Rawpixel.com 4, 83, Reinhold Leitner 39, Rich Carey 72, 72, 80, Richard Waters 72, 72, 80, Rob Kemp 87, Robbi 14, 24, 58, 68, 90, Ronnie Howard 55, Ronsmith 73, 77, 77, sangsiripech 22, 24, Sari ONeal 27, 27, Sashkin 33, Seaphotoart 77, Sergiy Bykhunenko 90, SkillUp 14, 24, 27, 36, 46, 49, 58, 68, 71, 80, 90, 93, smereka 43, son Photo 67, Stephen Mcsweeny 70, stockcreations 60, 68, StockImageFactory.com 68, stockphoto mania 38, 43, 46, 59, 59, 59, Stocksnapper 43, studio online 60, 61, 68, StudioSmart 41, suchalinee 11, sunlight19 83, Syda Productions 88, tanuha2001 67, Tatiana Popova 57, 61, 68, Tiplyashina Evgeniya 67, Tom Bird 41, TTstudio 49, UfaBizPhoto 33, urfin 16, usako 27, Valentyn Volkov 61, 79, Viktorl 22, 24, violetkaipa 33, VIS Fine Art 4, wavebreakmedia 67, 83, Winston Link/Shutterstock 28, 32, 86, Wire_man 64, 64, worradirek 87, Yeko Photo Studio 60, 61, 68, Yellow Cat 87, Zachary Dailey 77

Animation screen shots

Artwork by Lesley Danson/Bright Agency, production by Dardanele Studio

Illustrated by:

Barry Ablett/Beehive Illustration, pp.38 (bottom), 39 (top), 41 (bottom), 47(top), 48 (animals), 50, 51 (top dinosaurs), 53, 55 (dinosaurs), 57, 58, 59 (dinosaurs, goat), 70 (dinosaurs), 86 (dressing up box), 90 (bottom left), 92 (animals), 93 (seahorse); Constanza Basaluzzo/MB Artists, pp.8-9, 18-19, 20 (middle), 30, 31 (top), 40, 41 (top), 42 (story characters), 45 (top), 51 (dog), 52, 55 (story character), 59 (dog), 62, 63 (top), 66 (bottom), 74, 84, 85, 86 (story characters, lizard), 88; Julia Castaño/Bright Agency, p.94; Tamara Joubert and Daniela Geremia/Beehive Illustration, pp.23 (top), 38 (top); Daniel Limon/Beehive Illustration, pp.6, 7 (top, middle), 10, 12, 14, 17 (top), 20 (present), 27, 29 (bottom), 45 (middle), 55 (bottom), 69 (bottom), 72, 78, 89, 91 (bottom); Berta Maluenda/Bright Agency, pp.16, 20 (bottom), 25, 26, 55 (fox), 71, 87; Marina Martin/Bright Agency, pp.4, 15, 20 (top, numbers), 23 (bottom), 35 (bottom), 42, 45 (bottom), 55 (sheep), 60, 63 (middle), 65, 69 (top), 70 (food), 82, 83 (top), 86 (mask), 90 (top), 91 (top), 92 (costumes), 93 (mask); Lucy Neale/Bright Agency, pp.5, 17 (middle), 24, 39 (middle), 51 (middle), 56, 61, 73 (middle), 83 (middle), 90 (bottom right); Christos Skaltsas/Advocate Art, pp.7 (bottom), 11 (top), 21, 32, 33 (top), 47 (bottom), 51 (trees), 54, 55 (top), 66 (top), 73 (top), 75, 76, 80, 86 (dog), 86 (bottom), 92 (shrimp, fish); Ben Whitehouse/Bright Agency, pp.11 (bottom), 28, 29 (top, middle), 31 (bottom), 34, 35 (top), 36, 37, 43, 44, 48 (instruments), 51 (bottom), 64, 79, 93.

Cover Image: *Front:* **Pearson Education Ltd:** Jon Barlow